Advance Praise for
The Child with Autism at Home and in the Community

"*After giving a daylong* presentation in Louisiana last year, I went out to dinner with a group of mothers of children with autism. The conversation around the table was filled with laughter, down-home advice, support, and instant understanding—but mostly laughter. Each knew one another's children and bonded over the struggles the others were going through. What struck me most as I got to know these remarkable women was that they never forgot how to have fun.

"Kathy Labosh would have fit right into that group. Her practical advice, her positive philosophy, and her sense of humor shine through. She brings up topics that many parents worry about but hesitate to discuss. She offers ideas without making you feel guilty, because you know she has walked in your shoes. Her focus is not just on the child with autism, but also on the life of the family.

"Parents—if you can, find a group of friends to laugh and cry with. But if you are alone out there, take this little book to bed with you, and before you fall asleep, you will find at least one idea that will help you the next day as you live with and love your children with autism. And you will know that you are not alone any more."

Phyllis Kupperman, M.A., CCC-SLP
Executive Director/Founder
Center for Speech and Language Disorders
Elmhurst/Chicago, Illinois

"I have known Kathy and Timothy Labosh and their son Nicky, who is a student in the program under my supervision, for a year and a half. During that time, I have been impressed with Kathy's determination, her sensitivity and insight, and her ability to share practical and helpful information, based on real-life experiences, with families and professionals alike.

"I believe you will find this book useful. It is written with understanding; it is written with empathy; and it is from the heart. The nontechnical, down-to-earth style is direct, and the tips offered incorporate an in-depth knowledge of how children with autism learn. It respects the child and affirms each child's own learning style and uniqueness.

"This is a book that can be appreciated by families, professionals, and community providers. It not only affirms the right of all individuals to have access to their communities, but also illustrates how this can be done so all can benefit."

Richard Barbour, M.S., M.Ed.
Supervisor, Autism Support
Lancaster/Lebanon, PA IU 13

the Child with Autism

at Home & in the Community

Over 600 must-have tips for making home life and outings easier for everyone!

KATHY LABOSH *and* LANITA MILLER

FUTURE HORIZONS INC.
Arlington, Texas

 at Home and in the Community

All marketing and publishing rights guaranteed to and reserved by:

FUTURE HORIZONS INC.
721 W. Abram Street
Arlington, Texas 76013
800-489-0727
817-277-0727
817-277-2270 (fax)
E-MAIL: *info@FHautism.com*
www.FHautism.com

ISBN: 978-1-935274-20-9

Publisher's Cataloging-In-Publication Data
(Prepared by The Donohue Group, Inc.)
Labosh, Kathy.
  The child with autism at home & in the community / Kathy Labosh and LaNita Miller.
    p. ; cm. -- (The child with autism)
  Includes bibliographical references and index.
  ISBN: 978-1-935274-20-9
  1. Autistic children. 2. Autistic children--Behavior modification. 3. Parents of autistic children.
4. Autism in children--Popular works. I. Miller, LaNita. II. Title.
RJ506.A9 L23 2010
649/.154

Printed in the United States of America

*This book is dedicated to Tim Labosh and Bob Miller,
our husbands, whose fidelity, strength, and understanding
are the foundation of our happy homes.*

Acknowledgements

Thank you to the contributors and consultants who leant their support and expertise:

Diane Boomsma, F.I.A.C.P.
Registered Pharmacist

Peter J. Ross, D.M.D.
Pediatric Dentist

Timothy Labosh, M.D.
Family Practice Doctor

And thank you to Sam and Nicky Labosh. Your smiling faces and loving hearts have made me the happiest of mothers.

Table of Contents

Foreword

A Christmas party about nine years ago. It's families, mainly, maybe thirty people, with a lot of kids knocking about, and a lot of candles on the tables. I'm there in my capacity as grandma; we're all journalists, novelists, psychologists; we've all known each other one way or another for years. My grandson is running and playing, but he isn't running or playing with anyone else, and everyone in our family keeps a worried eye on him. "He marches to a different drummer," my stepmom has said about Dash. "He lives in his own little world."

Yes, that's true, and the family, for the last maybe four or five months, has been discussing just this, in rounds of increasingly futile-seeming conversations: "There isn't anything wrong with him." "There's definitely something wrong with him." "Why doesn't someone talk to his mother about it?" "Well, why don't YOU talk to his mother about it?" The truth is, nobody can get up the courage to talk to his mother about it. ("Well, she knows something's wrong, doesn't she?" "I don't know, have you talked to her about it?") Now tonight, my daughter Clara approaches the hostess of the party, who's a psychologist, old enough to be my daughter's mother. We've known her for years; she's wise, and warm, and extraordinarily decent. Clara asks her something, and I hear her say to Clara, "Maybe he has Asperger's." The kindest possible way to deliver a diagnosis of autism. I see Clara in the golden, candlelit glow of the party. I think I see her draw in a breath, hold one arm across her stomach, cross her other arm over to her opposite shoulder. Keeping her insides from flying out across the room.

And that's how it began for us—a family agony. I know that's not the good-sport way of putting it, but there's no point in lying either. It gets worse, and it gets better, and there are insults and there are setbacks and there are moments that are unbelievably amazing, but when it starts, it feels like agony, pure and simple. And there are people who assure that your autistic children are gifts from God, and that the Lord never gives you more than you can handle, and all that may be true, but in those first months, the agony is what you feel.

You've been thrust into a different world. You've got this child who may do any number of things: Spin scarves. Vocalize at the top of his voice, either in English or out of it. Escape. Then escape again. "Refuse" to meet your eyes. Withhold feces. Or spread his feces around the room, with glee. Not "hear" what you say. Not care what you say. The doctors say these children can't feel emotion, which I think is pretty clearly a great big lie. The truth is, the doctors don't know much about it, so far.

The first case of autism was only diagnosed in the late forties. Bruno Bettleheim, the self-appointed doctor and scientist who became autism's leading authority (who had been nothing more than a furniture salesman before the war), decided that autism must be the mothers' fault, and invented the term "refrigerator mothers," which haunted innocent mothers for years. He was dead wrong, of course, but by the time his career was finished, he had done irreparable damage. There are no accurate tests for autism. The diagnostic process takes weeks, sometimes longer, since medical people, being human beings, hesitate to be the ones to deliver bad news. Meanwhile, a family is sheltering and loving a child who sometimes can't stand human touch, or is terrified by a particular food, or can't "play" with other kids, and on and on.

In most states, parents of autistic kids are entitled to services. But what kind of services? What is needed for these children? How are they best treated? I know I've been to dozens of meetings, where specialists put together programs with speech therapy, social skills therapy, physical therapy, and then the almost literally countless activities that sometimes help children who have autism, and sometimes don't. Horseback riding. White water rafting (Really!). Surfing. Musical comedy groups (which helped Dash immensely, letting him participate in groups, learning to sing, and—more touching than I can say—accepting applause).

Some things work and some things don't. As a book critic for the *Washington Post*, I became a de facto expert on autism and books about autism. My family and I learned that Nick Hornby, the marvelous English novelist, has a child with autism, and is doing great work with kids over in England. And that John Travolta had a child with autism whom he loved beyond words, but he had to deny his son's condition for some time because of religious considerations. We met all kinds of wonderful children and their great parents—a boy named Noel, who's been in love with Dash for years and can only speak in questions: "Will Dash wear his blue shirt tomorrow?" Children who wept easily, and spoke intermittently or never, children who smiled or danced or banged their heads against the walls ... sometimes they "improved," sometimes they didn't. But parents learned, because they had to, how to become "autism parents."

A whole sub-genre of books sprang up—autobiographies by mothers of children with autism. These books were full of anguish, but often held seeds of various victories. A mother who "cured" her son by buying him a very beautiful dog. Another woman who had three children, and said that the rest of her life will be lived in the world of autism. Another woman who seemed to have cured herself of depression and despair when she saw her child up on a stage for the first time.

But there's nothing in the canon like Kathy Labosh's book. I can't say enough how helpful this book will be to the parents and grandparents of children with autism. There's very little philosophy here—except the duly stated hypothesis that yes, these children really ARE a gift from God, and that we wouldn't have them if we couldn't handle them. But after that, this book is made up of what to do, pure and simple. If your child is driving you crazy, just step outside for a minute; the world looks a little more serene from outside the house. (And you can always hear what's going on inside.) But right next to that suggestion, Remember to take your house keys with you! Because they can lock you out. I laughed when I read that, recalling an evening when I babysat Dash, he scrambled under the bed, and I creaked on in after him—and got stuck there. We had to wait until his parents got home.

For that pesky problem of them never looking at you, Kathy suggests: put an M&M between your eyes. Well, sure! Why didn't I think of that? The problem of where and how they focus their eyes is a real one. Not being looked at freaks "normal" people out; they feel slighted, and project that emotion on to the child—in just the same way that "experts" have said that kids with autism don't feel emotion. What emotion would YOU feel if some loudmouthed joker jammed his head down in front of your face and ordered you to say the alphabet for the two hundredth time, when, odds are, you've known the alphabet for years, but physically aren't able to articulate it? You'd give that guy the cold shoulder, and he'd blame it all on you.

Kathy tries not to get into this stuff. She just gives you hundreds of tips to make your life easier, and your child's life easier. That whole feces thing, for instance. When your child has seen fit to decorate himself, the room, the walls, the floors, the draperies, with feces, she suggests coming at him from behind, placing your hands under his arms, and lifting him into the tub, because for some reason the armpits are the last parts to be decorated. She reminds us to take a cloth to the doorknobs, in case we've forgotten. She suggests dropping just a little Drano into the drains, since feces may get lodged down somewhere with hair and other goo and soon your whole home will smell faintly like a latrine. All this material is priceless stuff, and—no offense to the lady who bought the dog for her child—these suggestions here will actually do you a world of good. While you're pondering why God had singled you out for this test, you can also take your mind off the whole thing by affixing an M&M between your eyes.

Let me tell you a last little bit about Dash, my own dear grandson. He's killingly handsome, and very sweet natured. He has always seemed to me to get the joke. But his eating habits were strange. His vocabulary very limited. He loved—still loves—to spin scarves and necklaces. He rubs his nose until his upper lip bleeds when he feels sad. Countless times, his teachers have told us he's "uneducable." Except that about six months ago, his parents took him to see just one more tutor—this one in "augmentative communication"—and by the end of the first hour, Dash had typed out that he lived in CALIFORNIA, and that his favorite subjects in school were MATH and SPELLING. And that he liked to JUMP on the TRAMPOLINE. So it turns out that right now we're living with multiple versions of Dash: the darling little autistic boy who loves to be tickled (and Kathy's suggestions for a Tickle Monster here are essential), a somewhat cranky, extraordinarily intelligent dude who can spell "liaison" correctly and knows what it means, a formerly "uneducable" person who scores "proficient" in Math and English, and a person who can write to his mom on Mother's Day, "Everyone likes you as a friend because you are the prettiest mom."

I say this not to promise that your kid with autism will get "better." He already is "better." I say it to encourage you to take these days with your child one step at a time, to read Kathy Labosh's book like it was Dr. Spock's, to approach each task with as brave a heart as you can muster, to hold on to the belief that your kid is watching you with the purest, strangest, most unique intelligence. He gets the joke, I assure you! And you might as well get it too.

CAROLYN SEE
Author of *Making a Literary Life*

Preface

This book was written out of empathy for families living with autism. I do mean families. A particular child may have the symptoms, but the entire family is affected. In my own case, both of my children—Sam, age seventeen, and Nicky, age fourteen—have autism to varying degrees. I do not know what it is like to raise a normal child.

My son Sam's diagnosis of autism caught me unprepared. I looked back on all the missed signs. Cherished memories were revisited in the new light of autism. Future plans were grieved. A desperate search for knowledge ensued. I wanted it to be within my power to cure it. I did not need for my son to be a superstar; I only desired a level of normalcy. Even that modest dream seemed cruelly unreachable.

In the midst of all the despair, I also felt an intense love and devotion toward my son. I searched with hope for every small improvement and marveled at his determination and his joy. He was and is, for me, a perfect child.

I knew his brother, Nicky, had autism long before anyone else did. I watched him carefully. He did not respond to his name. The feel of clothes against his skin and the weight of blankets on his small body would make him scream. He never pointed at what he wanted, and he would cuddle with any woman who vaguely resembled me. I knew inside, but I would have to wait until he was old enough for others to know, too.

I thought my experiences with Sam would help me with Nicky, and they did, but not as much as I had hoped. Although Sam had minimal sensory issues and was verbal, Nicky had many sensory issues and was nonverbal and low functioning. I had to learn new ways of dealing with autism. Every new issue had to be thought through. Books on typical childhood development did not address my problems, except to advise seeing a doctor.

I compare my life's journey with autism to a hike up the Appalachian Trail. My ability to complete the journey with joy and satisfaction depends upon my ability to take care of myself physically, to prepare mentally for the hard stretches, to use the right tools to make the trek easier, and to have a good support system in place. But more than anything else, what I have needed is a trail to follow and a map to help me when I got lost.

My book is a tool that can help you in practical ways on your journey. I have not reached the end of the journey, but I have learned from my time wandering lost in the woods. My desire is to spare you that. *The Child with Autism* is a compilation of my best advice on how to keep yourself and your marriage together, how to discipline your children, how to teach them to be self-sufficient and contributing members of your family. I have even included sections on toys and activities that my children love, to help you make your home a happy one.

Over the years, I have also learned many strategies for taking my children out into the community. Much of the wisdom contained in this book was gained through my own trial and error. Some of the tips I learned through hindsight; others came from professionals who work with children who have autism. My desire is for these strategies to serve as trail markers for you as you venture out into the community with your own child in tow.

Sam, our older son, is high-functioning and has always been a joy. I previously credited this to my parenting skills. Then I had Nicky, who is low-functioning and prone to destroying things. Some children are more difficult than others. If your child is difficult, there are things you can do to improve his behavior in the community.

Some of my tips are unconventional. Families living with autism face many challenges not ordinarily found in typical families. We often change our customary behavior to adapt to the needs of our loved ones. For instance, when Sam and Nicky were young and nonverbal, I could not feed them at the table. Sam would take one bite every couple of minutes while Nicky would gobble his food and anyone else's within reach. In order to keep both boys fed and calm, I needed to feed them separately, in their rooms. That was the structure I needed for my family to function.

I let an early intervention class teach my children to eat at a table, and then transferred those skills to our home. There will likely be behaviors that your child will learn more easily in a school setting. Embrace the help. Often the child is alone in a room with an aide whose job it is to work one-on-one with them. That person gets to leave at the end of the day. Parents of children with autism can't do that. Do not feel that you are a failure as a parent because others can teach your child things that you cannot.

I have asked LaNita Miller, my children's first teacher, and the person who taught them and many other children with autism these skills, to share some of these tips. I would like to claim that I am the super-parent who can do it all, but it is better to be someone who realizes her limitations. To survive, you have to recognize your need for others.

The roots of the Community portion of the book reach back to a time when I felt despair. Despite an early diagnosis and early treatment, Nicky was doing poorly in his Autism Early Intervention Class. Skills that he mastered one day would be forgotten the next.

In the fall of 2000, I got a glimpse into how Nicky learned best. I took my sons down to Emmitsburg, Maryland, to see the autumn colors. We stopped at a mountainside shrine, and Nicky jumped out of the car and raced a half mile to where there was a statue with a fountain and a pool. I was dumbfounded. We had been there only once, five months earlier, and Nicky had remembered the location of the fountain after seeing only the parking lot.

A few weeks later, I visited a friend I had not seen in years. She lived in a townhouse in a row of identical houses. Nicky ran to the correct townhouse, hurried up the steps, and went straight to the trampoline he remembered. My son, who knew only a few words receptively and could speak none, had a phenomenal memory for where he had been and what he had done there.

I then did what some would consider unthinkable. I dropped his classroom days down to three, and took him out into the community. With the assistance of Amy Hess, Nicky's Therapeutic Staff Support, I taught him how to behave. A good helper in these endeavors is priceless! Together we explored the grocery store, fast-food restaurants, farms, zoos, and the shopping mall. We photographed many of the things he saw on those trips, and gave the photographs to his autism class. Nicky's receptive language grew as he connected the words he heard with the pictures of what he remembered.

He still speaks no words as of 2011, but he has maturity and a worldly savvy that allows him to handle many social situations. He is back in his autism class full-time, and is now learning his academics. I firmly believe his exposure to the community at large will continue to help him learn for years to come.

Please note: The only time I could work with Nicky one-on-one was while his brother was in school. You need to evaluate what works best for your family.

Most of the hints and strategies in this book were gleaned from all of these experiences. Sam, our older son, enjoys all the activities in this book as well. Their behavior is not perfect—but then, neither is the behavior of typical children.

Good luck in your endeavors. I pray that this book helps your family enjoy a full and active life in the community.

KATHY LABOSH

Part One

The Child with Autism at Home

Chapter 1

The Attic: Your Mental Attitude

A happy home begins with you. All children—and especially those with autism—are sensitive to their parents' moods. A shouting match between you and your spouse may seem like "just a normal argument" to you, but it can terrify a child with autism. As a result, he may act out for days or weeks after the event, and some children will avoid for a lifetime anything they connect with the traumatic event. All parents have arguments, but if you stay calm and deal with negative emotions in positive ways, you can actually strengthen the family unit by modeling the mature way to deal with conflict.

- Make sure you get adequate sleep; when you are tired you have less control over your emotions and may make poor decisions. *(If the reason you don't get enough sleep is that your child has problems with sleep, please refer to* The Child's Bedroom *chapter.)*

- Decide what is *truly necessary* for you to accomplish right this minute, or even today. For example, don't sacrifice your sleep to do a load of laundry. Your sleep is truly necessary for your well-being; doing the laundry right now is not.

- Take a daily vitamin. Our bodies and brains need certain vitamins and minerals to function optimally. Most of us don't get enough of these nutrients from food.

- Eat raw apples to stay awake during the day. They work like a stimulant. Don't ask me why; just try it.

- Eat some protein with your breakfast: yogurt, bacon, an egg, etc. Eating just a sugary snack can cause your emotions—and your energy levels—to go up and down like a roller coaster during the day.

- Get a treadmill (check out garage sales if you can't afford a new one—many of the exercise machines you will find at garage sales have hardly been used). Stress releases hormones in your body that cause the "fight or flight" response. If you don't want to fight and you can't leave the house because the kids are in it, a treadmill gives you a way to release stress in a healthy way. It also makes you stronger!

- Learn and practice stretching exercises like Tai Chi or yoga. Tension causes your muscles to "knot up" uncomfortably, often in your neck and shoulders, as well as in other locations. A masseur or masseuse can work those knots out, but the cost can be prohibitive. Taking a class in Tai Chi or yoga costs much less, and once you learn how to perform these exercises you can do them at home for free.

- Take deep breaths. This causes physical changes in your body that relax it.

- Don't expect too much of yourself. There's a limit to how much you can do in a day without denying yourself rest, fun, relaxation, and some "alone time." Also, the more hurried (and harried) you are, the more likely you are to lose your temper.

- Write to-do lists when the children are sleeping. It's easier to focus when you're not wondering what the kids are doing in the next room, or dealing with the current crisis.

- Frustration builds when you are constantly interrupted. You can't prevent interruptions, but you can plan ahead for them! Break down your chores into small steps: 1) collect laundry; 2) sort it; 3) put it in the washer; 4) add detergent, etc.; 5) turn on the washer. You can break down most tasks in this manner. It's less stressful to have a small task interrupted than when it is an entire procedure.

- Whenever you see something that needs to be done, add it to your to-do list. This tricks your mind into thinking you've actually done something about it.

- Limit how much news you watch. News reports focus on disasters, wars, mayhem, disease ... you don't need the added stress.

- Read the newspaper instead. You can at least choose which parts of it you want to read, and when you want to read them. If you're interrupted, it's easy to pick up where you left off.

- Get TiVo or record your favorite shows *as you watch them*. That way, if you're interrupted, you can still catch up on what you missed.

- Write letters to God. Pour out all the anger, frustration, and negative emotions that you feel toward Him and others. Ask for help and forgiveness. Then tear the letter up.

- Join autism chat rooms where you can talk with others in similar situations.

- Call old friends to stay connected to your emotional support system. Some of these friendships will taper off, but others will deepen.

- Take an interest in your friends' lives; don't just use them as receptacles into which you unload your stress.

- Be careful whom you call when you are really upset; make sure it's someone who's sympathetic and supportive. Not everyone understands your situation.

- If you need a break but can't leave the house, step outside for a few minutes. You can still hear everything that's going on inside.

- Take your keys when you step outside; children playing with the inside knob could accidentally lock the door.

- View your children as gifts from God. They teach patience, kindness, and selflessness. They were given to you because God believes in you.

- Grieve the future that you hoped for, and find joy in the little things. The only place you can find joy is where you are; the only time you can find joy is now.

- Focus on what your child can do, rather than what he cannot do.

- Realize that it will take repetition for your child to learn things. You are establishing new neural pathways in his brain. This happens only through repetition.

- Don't get upset with the pace of your child's progress; it's not his fault he has autism. Expressions of frustration tend to slow down learning. And the child might be afraid to try that activity again, because he associates it with getting in trouble.

- Stop feeling guilty. It's not your fault, any more than it is your child's fault, that he has autism. Autism is a worldwide phenomenon, and no one yet knows what causes it. You cannot hold yourself responsible.

- Recognize that you are never going to be able to do everything you "should." No one can.

- Find ways to make your child smile. The beauty of his smile will warm your soul on your saddest days.

- Keep your sense of humor. Your attitude can make all the difference in your ability to cope.

- Repeat often to your child: "It's a good thing you're so cute!"

Chapter 2

The Master Bedroom

Autism puts the wedding vow, "For better or for worse," to the test. There is a shift of focus from the couple to the child with autism. So much energy is spent trying to help him and make sure that he and the house survive intact that the marriage's needs often take a backseat. There are some small but meaningful things you can do to support your spouse. These tips are suggestions—not a list of demands to present to your spouse.

- Thank your spouse often for things you may have taken for granted. Going to work, watching the kids, and putting food on the table are necessary for a family's survival. Feeling unappreciated is a major cause of marital discontent. Make your spouse's life brighter simply by noticing what he or she does for the family.

- Tell your spouse what you admire about him or her. We all have our flaws, but we also have our strengths. When we are feeling down and inadequate, it's good to be reminded of our strengths and how far we've come.

- Each spouse should have at least one night of the week they can count on to be on their own. It's important to have a break from the demands of work and home. These nights need to be something they can plan on, look forward to, and count on.

- Join a group that has nothing to do with autism, and everything to do with *you*. It could be a bowling league, the church choir, a bridge club, a sports team, or an exercise class. It is there that you can have fun and meet people who may become friends, or even part of your support system.

- Have friends over to watch sports or play cards. Let your friends meet your children in their home environment. Allow your friends to get to know you as a couple, even if they don't see you together all of the time.

- Check with the local Office of Mental Retardation to learn if it has "family driven funds" that can be used by your family for respite care. They may supply you with a list of respite care providers. If you do use their services, enjoy your break!

- Arrange to have regular time away from the kids as a couple. You will be a different person when you are relieved of the responsibility for the children. You need to see that, underneath it all, the marriage is still intact.

- Realize that your child's autism may have a genetic component. You and/or your spouse may be mildly autistic. That person's ability to cope with certain stresses might be impaired. You need to be patient with yourself, and with your spouse.

- State the obvious. It may not be obvious to everyone.

- Be patient with repetition. People often do not remember whom they told what. It is better to be told something a couple of times rather than not be told at all!

- Deal with unresolved pain. Avoiding a topic only deepens the pain and prolongs the healing process.

- Understand that your spouse is not Superman or Superwoman. Your emotional needs are not going to be fully met by your spouse. They do love you, but one person just cannot meet all the demands that are placed on them.

- Redefine love in terms of commitment rather than romantic ideals. The children will probably eat the candles and destroy the flowers. Love is about doing what it takes to keep the family on solid ground and caring about what happens to the other person.

- Watch your assumptions and question them. Many arguments start because someone misunderstood what was really going on and incorrectly "filled in the blanks."

- Apologize. It's the quickest way to end an argument and get an apology in return. People will listen to you more carefully and respect you more if they know they have been heard, and that you care that they were hurt.

- Ask for help in a positive manner. Say "Could you open the door for me, please?" instead of "Can't you see that I need help with the door?" The first approach affirms your spouse; the second tears them down. Your spouse can't read your mind. Their thoughts may be on their own problems. Respect that.

- Say "Did you get a chance to. . ." instead of "Did you...." This acknowledges your awareness that your spouse has many responsibilities and pressures.

- Stress and sex are physically incompatible. If you are going to have sex, you both need to relax first. A backrub, a hot shower, or nonsexual physical affection needs to come first.

- Find ways of making physical contact with your spouse during the day. A hug, a kiss, or a hand on the shoulder will bind you together and reassure your spouse that the two of you are in this together.

- Avoid things that will unnecessarily add stress to your family life. Adultery, drugs, or alcohol abuse can easily founder a marriage.

- Beware of well-meaning but toxic friends who sympathize in a way that encourages resentment toward your spouse. Find a friend who understands that a broken marriage is a lifetime of pain for all involved—especially for the kids.

- Do not mention your friends' opinions during an argument. Your spouse really doesn't need to know what someone else thinks of him or her. That person has only a one-sided, biased view of the problems. Your spouse will probably end up forgiving you, but will probably never again feel comfortable around your friend.

- Assume that, no matter how inadequate the results, both of you are really doing your best. Forgive any shortcomings, because they truly exist on both sides.

Chapter 3

The Child's Bedroom

In order for you *to get* adequate sleep, your *child* needs to get adequate sleep. Most sleep problems are actually sensory issues: your child may be cold, hungry, or hyperactive. His blanket, comforter, sheets, or pajamas could be uncomfortable, or he may be experiencing a floating feeling when he lies down. It's a matter of trial and error to discover what the problem is.

- Remove the tags from pajamas (and all clothing), and buy only "plain" pajamas—appliqués, raised lettering or pictures, embroidery, etc., can feel uncomfortable, as can some buttons and zippers.

- Buy plain sheets; he may be afraid of the animals or characters printed on them.

- Wash blankets, sheets, pajamas (and all clothing) with detergent that is free of perfumes, dyes, bleach, and bleach alternatives.

- If your child tends to kick his bedclothes off during the night, wait until *after* he is asleep before covering him with a blanket.

- Buy pajamas that have "feet" and a zipper. If your child knows how to undo the zipper, get a larger size, cut off the "feet," and put the pajamas on backwards, with the zipper in the back.

- Cut off the arms and legs of the pajamas for use during summertime.
- If your child will not tolerate either pajamas or blankets, raise the temperature in the house.
- Switch to flannel sheets. They are softer than traditional sheets, and warmer in the wintertime. Kids will sometimes accept them even if they don't like regular sheets.
- Place pillows on the floor around the edge of the bed. If your child falls out of bed, he will land on the pillows. Sometimes kids don't even wake up when this happens!
- Relax an upset child by firmly stroking his legs and feet. This will give him sensory input to focus on.
- Install a ceiling fan with lights. Use the fan during the summer to keep the child cool. (And the fan's lights are hard for your child to break!)
- Watching the ceiling fan rotate can be relaxing for some children.
- Have him sleep in a mini pup tent if he likes small, enclosed spaces.
- If your child likes to sleep on the floor, give him a very firm mattress. He may be experiencing a floating feeling, and not getting enough sensory input from his body to know where he is in space.
- Tuck him in very tightly. It helps him feel secure, and helps keep him from falling out of bed. It also increases the sensory input to his brain.
- Put a TV that is connected only to a VCR/DVD player in the child's bedroom. The TV should be at your child's eye level when he is going to sleep. Place it on the floor if he sleeps on the floor, or at bed-height or a little higher if he is sleeping on a bed.

- Do not turn off the TV, but do turn off the DVD player when he goes to sleep so there is only static on the TV (this only works if the TV is not connected to anything but the DVD player). When they are tired or overtired, they can get very upset, and even more active. If you can stop them to watch TV, it gives their body a chance to go to sleep. (This isn't recommended for typical children.)

- Play a movie that your child enjoys, and has seen many times before. He will be able to close his eyes and follow along in his imagination.

- Turn the volume down very low, so he will have to be quiet in order to hear the video.

- Do not turn off the TV. It will switch over to static after the movie ends, because the TV is not connected to anything but the VCR. The "white noise" of the static will prevent other sounds from waking him up.

- Wake your child up in the morning the same way. Turn on a favorite video and turn the volume up. It will wake him up slowly, and in a good mood.

- If even a video is too stimulating, try using soft music instead.

- Do not let your child nap for long periods during the day. It increases the chance that he will wake up in the middle of the night, ready to play.

- Let your child stay up until he is sleepy, and then put him to bed. It will help him associate the bed with sleep. If you put him to bed before he is sleepy, he will want to play, and a battle will ensue. Then he won't want to go to bed at all, because he will associate going to bed with fighting.

- Don't let him sleep anywhere but in the bedroom, preferably on the bed.

- Gradually move back the time your child goes to bed. Start by putting him to bed ten minutes earlier.

- If your child enjoys books, read to him. The goal is to keep him in bed, quietly, long enough that he will fall asleep. If the book is one he knows well, he can follow the story with his eyes closed.

- If the child has been sleeping in your bed, move him into his own bed. Lie down beside him and let him hold your hand or hair, so he can feel secure.

- Sit beside the bed on the floor. Let him "snuggle" with you by holding on to your arm or hand.

- Sit beside the bed, just out of reach. Stay with him till he falls asleep.

- Turn out the light if the child continues to get out of bed. Most children with autism don't like the dark. Turn the lights back on only if he gets back into bed.

- Do not leave the lights on overnight. It isn't good for the child's eyes. You can leave a light on in the hall, or let the TV provide minimal light.

- Get melatonin made into a flavored lozenge at a compounding pharmacy; it is not a sleeping pill, but it will help your child feel sleepy. The body naturally produces melatonin when preparing for sleep, but your child may not be producing enough of it.

- If nothing will get your child to sleep, ask your pediatrician for a prescription medicine.

- Warn your child five to ten minutes before you begin the bedroom routine. It will give him time to stop what he is doing, and mentally prepare for the transition. (This is also useful at bathtime and other transitions.)

Chapter 4

The Corner

Children with autism have a reputation for having disciplinary problems. However, such problems are often due to the fact that they don't understand what it is you want them to do—or you don't understand what *they* want. Requests must be phrased clearly, and any tasks you are asking them to perform must be within their skill level.

- Start with the assumption that your child did not understand what you wanted him to do. Make your response a teaching experience rather than a punishment.

- Pause after making your request. Give the child a minute or more to process what you are asking him for. People often underestimate how long it takes for a child with autism to process a request or learn a task.

- Let your child show you what he wants by offering your hand and letting him take you where he wants to go. Release his hand if he is trying to get away from you. See what he wants. My son once fought very hard to get his hand out of mine, only to go to the other hand. My rings had been hurting his hand!

- After you have let him communicate what he wants, say either yes or no. He will accept your answer better if he knows he's been heard.

- Let your *no's* sound like "NO." Say it in a firm voice, but without shouting—which can just add to your child's anxiety. Children with autism have a hard time discerning emotions. They need clear signals.

- Let your *no **mean** no.* Children with autism can be extremely persistent. If your child continues to disobey, either he or the prohibited object needs to be removed from the situation. Expecting your child to exercise self-control when the desired object is in view and within reach is simply asking too much of him.

- Think before you say *no* if you know you are probably going to change your mind. If you do decide to change your mind, reframe your answer. For example, "No, we can't go to the pool now, but we can go at six o'clock."

- Let your *yes **mean** yes.* If you said you would go to the pool at six o'clock, GO. At six o'clock.

- Make him apologize to everyone involved with his inappropriate conduct. For example, if he spat at another child at camp, he should apologize to the camp counselor, the camp nurse, the other child's aide, and the child at whom he spat. Learning to say, "I'm sorry" is an important social skill.

- Have him make restitution to the injured party. For example, if your child's favorite snack is Skittles, he should give them to the child he spat at.

- Have your child correct his mistakes. If he took all your flatware out of the drawers, he must replace it. You may have to physically show him how to do this by placing your hand over his and doing it together.

- Have him clean up his own messes. If your child spills juice on the floor, have him get a paper towel and clean it up.

- Be cross when pointing out a serious error, but be effusive with praise when your child is correcting it.

- If your child breaks something, hold the object in front of his face when you are talking to him. This will give him a visual clue as to what he did wrong.

- If your child throws a temper tantrum in public, do nothing. Wait until he gets it out of his system, and then continue with whatever you were going to do.

- Have some business cards printed that say something like "My child has autism. I'm doing the best I can. If you want more information about autism, please contact the Autism Society of America at 1-800-3AUTISM." Pass the card to curious onlookers and continue to focus on your child.

- Learn the difference between a temper tantrum and a panic attack. Remove a panicked child from the stressor. It is extremely important that your child is able to trust you to protect him from perceived threats. You will need to slowly desensitize him to feared objects.

- If your child throws a temper tantrum at home, send him to his room. He can throw as horrific a tantrum as he wants, but you do not have to see it or hear it.

- Reverse the locks on your child's door so that the locking mechanism is on the outside of the door. This prevents the child from locking himself inside the room.

- Time-out minutes should correspond to the age of the child—usually lasting one minute for each year of his age. Let him have a timer so he will know when his time out is over.

- If the child refuses to stay where you put him for the time out, then lock him in his room for the appropriate amount of time. You will let the child out when the timer goes off, regardless of how he is behaving. If he is still acting up or acts out again, you can put him back in his room, but a nonverbal child will not understand if you keep increasing his time out because he is misbehaving. He will have a better chance of understanding if he keeps getting sent into his room and is not released until the timer sounds.

- As an alternative, you can apply the ten-second rule. After the time out is over, he has to be quiet for ten seconds before he can get out of his room. Start counting to ten out loud. Every time he acts out, start over at "one."

- This is important: *Apply discipline in a clear, consistent manner.*

- If the child is stuck in a repetitive action, count down the number of times he can do something. Say, "Okay. Three more times, two more times, one more time. That's it. Come give me a hug. Now go find something else to do." This prepares him mentally for stopping. It is also a valuable skill he can use later in life.

- Make the countdown a positive experience. A negative experience will only add to the stress and the need to do something compulsively. You could try letting him do the countdown with you.

- Try Tylenol if your child engages in self-injurious behavior like biting himself or hitting himself. If the Tylenol stops the behavior, look for the cause of physical pin. Tooth pain, earaches, or headaches are all possibilities. If he does it frequently for no apparent reason, ask your doctor to check for seizure activity. Tell the doctor or dentist about your observations.

- Remove objects of obsession from sight if they are inappropriate or affecting his quality of life. You cannot discipline an obsession away. You may be able to return the objects at a later date—but don't be too hasty!

- Write out rules for a child who can read, or use pictures if he cannot. Children with autism are visual learners, and they are more likely to remember a written note than spoken directions.

- Tell him what a good child he is! Children with autism live for praise, and they can be easily crushed. They will live up to—or down to—the way you see them.

- Find things that your child is doing right, and praise him mightily! A child needs to understand that it is possible to please you. They will repeat the things that reward them. If you pay close attention, you'll likely find that your child is actually good *most of the time*. If you are always angry with him, his "reward" might be to get back at you!

- Make sure your child has adequate food and sleep. Tired and hungry children are more likely to act out.

- Figure out why your child is performing a particular behavior. He may be able to get the same result in a more appropriate way.

- Calm yourself if your child is upset. He will never be calmer than you are, and he will often mirror your emotions.

- Hug and kiss your child often. Happy children do not act out as much as unhappy children do.

Chapter 5

The Family Room

There are a number of enjoyable activities and projects that you can do with your child. These play activities stimulate his senses and provide interactive play with family members.

- Run scarves through your child's hands and around his neck. It tickles and has a silky feel.
- Flap the scarves; children like to see the colors and the fabric move.
- Cover a table with a protective paper and let your child do finger painting. He can make handprints, or just rub his hands over the paper.
- Paint with shaving cream on black paper. It has a nice smell and texture to it.
- Bury small prizes in a box of dried beans. Let your child dig through the beans to find the prize.
- Seal the box of beans with tape, and use it as a noisemaker your child can shake.
- Hide trinkets inside a ball of non-toxic modeling clay, and have your child manipulate the clay until he finds the object.

- Fill a dishpan full of warm water and dishwashing bubbles. Place it on your deck, patio, or balcony. Let him splash and wash various waterproof toys. He has fun, and the toys get cleaned.

- Give him sponges to fill with water and then squeeze dry.

- Let your fingers walk up your child's body from his toes to the top of his head.

- Blow on his belly.

- Walk slowly toward your child with your fingers wiggling, ready to tickle him. Chase him around the house until you catch him and tickle him.

- Tickle him just under his ears, under his chin, under his arms, on his belly, behind his knees, and on the bottom of his feet.

- Tickle him with feathers or feather dusters.

- Make an art project with glitter and glue; kids love shiny glitter.

- Shake pom-poms over his head or on his belly. Let him play with the pom-poms. They make an interesting sound, and they tickle.

- Have him run and jump on bubble wrap. Everyone loves to pop those bubbles!

- Roll and bounce your child on a large exercise ball.

- Teach him to put his hands out to stop his forward momentum on the ball. Children with autism often do not have that skill and will bang their heads. This is a very useful skill to have if they trip.

- Wrap him in a blanket and have two people swing him.

- Cover him with a blanket and tickle him through the blanket.

- Give strong hugs. Deep pressure feels very good to children with autism.

- Imitate his happy noise. Try to start a conversation with your child using his happy noise.

Chapter 6

The Playroom

Everyone wants to know what presents to give children with autism for special occasions (birthdays, holidays). Toys with high sensory input that require little or no manual dexterity are good. Many children with autism have a passion for letters and numbers. Others have a fascination for a particular object. Know your child's passion and work with it. The following is a list of toys most children with autism will like.

- Magnadoodles—It's easier for your child to draw with a magnetic pen than with a pencil or a crayon.
- Mini-trampoline—children with autism love to bounce! Supervise the jumping so they don't fall on something that could hurt them.
- Sit 'n' Spin for children who like to twirl
- Nerf balls for children who like to throw things
- Vibrating ball—They love the way it shakes.
- Spinning toys
- Wind-up toys
- Toy cars
- Koosh balls and animals

- Play-Doh—It has a good texture and is easy to manipulate.
- Crayons (make sure they're non-toxic, as they are often eaten)
- Silly Putty
- Books that make sounds
- Calculators—for children who love numbers
- Easy readers—for children who are learning to speak
- Videos and DVDs
- Flashlights
- Viewmasters
- Kaleidoscopes
- Snow globes
- Slinky—It won't last long, but your child will love it!
- Stress balls—balls that you can squeeze or mold
- Squeaky toys
- Beanie Babies
- Floppy stuffed animals
- Gumby or other one-piece dolls (action figures are quickly dismembered)
- Talking Dora the Explorer
- Tickle-Me Elmo
- Teletubbies or other favorite cartoon characters
- Tracking beads—They like to push the beads on the convoluted wires.
- Large Legos
- Simple wooden inset puzzles
- Glitter wands

Chapter 7

The Music Room

Some children are quite gifted with musical instruments; other children just like to bang on anything that makes noise. Music is a good way of introducing information into their minds. Many children will recall words and phrases that were sung to them.

- Piano—Let your child play on the keys. Try lessons if he shows an avid interest. The Suzuki method teaches them to play by ear. The traditional methods teach them to read notes. Determine which method is best for your child.

- Maracas—They are easy to handle and make noise while a child is bouncing.

- Tambourine—This instrument can be used with one or two hands. Teach your child to bang the tambourine against his other hand.

- Rhythm sticks—similar to the clapping motion

- Electronic keyboards—See Piano

- Bells—simple to use

- Rainsticks—They mimic the sound of rain when they are moved.

- Karaoke—Some children love to hear their voice through a microphone.
- Make up silly songs about things you want to teach him.

Chapter 8

The Kitchen

The kitchen is probably the most angst-filled room in the house. Children with autism are frequently very picky eaters, and researchers are always coming up with new things for you to stop feeding your child. Children with autism sometimes have digestive problems. Some children can be helped by a gluten- and casein (dairy)-free diet. Please note: This is not medical advice, and you should consult your physician regarding dietary questions and other medical issues.

- Do the "giggles test" to determine if your child might do well on the gluten-free, casein-free diet. Feed your child any grain-and-cheese mixture: pizza, macaroni and cheese, or a grilled cheese sandwich. If he gets the giggles shortly thereafter, he might not be digesting the food properly.

- Check for diarrhea the next day. If your child is not digesting gluten or dairy properly, it can result in diarrhea or constipation.

- Try this diet if your child throws tantrums on a regular basis.

- Give the diet a try for three months, and be on the lookout for any noticeable changes.

- Gluten-free and dairy-free foods can be found in health-food stores and on the Internet.

- Snacks children with autism often enjoy are: cheese-flavored crackers (like Goldfish), cheese curls, Swedish fish, gummy bears, Smarties, raisins, chewing gum, pretzels, Mike and Ike Candy, Jell-O and Mini M&Ms (Some of these snacks do contain gluten or casein.)

- Use the one-bite method to introduce new foods. If he takes one bite, he can have a piece of his favorite snack. Alternate bites until the plate is empty.

- If your child enjoys salty snacks, try foods like ham or bacon with a high salt content first (obviously, not for those on a Kosher diet).

- Give raw carrots to your child when his molars are coming in. They like to bite down hard on things during this process.

- Introduce ketchup. If your child likes it, try adding it to new foods that you are introducing.

- Introduce your child to Popsicles. You can use them as an ice pack for the mouth when he is teething or molars are coming in, or to rehydrate a child who can't keep anything down.

- Some children with touch sensitivities have problems with metal spoons and forks. If your child won't eat with metal utensils, try plastic ones.

- Ask an occupational therapist for adapted utensils. They are often easier to manipulate than "grown-up" ones.

- Dip the utensil in your child's favorite juice. This will give him practice accepting the utensil before you try to feed him solid food on it.

- Dip the utensil in peanut butter or yogurt (not for those on a dairy-free diet). These foods will coat the utensil, increasing the odds of successful eating.

- Give non-preferred foods before family time, when you can devote your full attention to feeding your child. Make sure your child is hungry before offering non-preferred foods.

- Give preferred foods as part of family mealtime. This will keep family meals enjoyable.

- Use a cushion disk or doughnut to help your child stay in his seat.

- Use a booster chair with arms or an adult chair with arms. Push the chair in, so the arms are under the table.

- Use a timer to show your child how long you want him to sit. Increase the time gradually. Be realistic about how long you expect a young child to sit.

- When the timer goes off, reward his success with a favorite activity.

- Pay attention to appropriate behavior; ignore inappropriate behavior.

- Save preferred activities for time at the table after the food is eaten.

- In packed lunches, use fold-top sandwich bags that can be opened easily.

- Slightly tear each package to make it easier for him to open it.

- Unscrew each bottle, and then retighten it just enough so the contents won't spill out. This allows your child to open the bottle easily, without making a mess.

Chapter 9

The Study

Both high-functioning and low-functioning children need help building vocabulary and learning concepts. High-functioning children who are mainstreamed into the school system often have trouble studying for tests because the material is geared toward typical learners.

The first fourteen tips will help you prepare a high-functioning child for classroom tests, and they can also be adapted for the lower-functioning child. The final nine tips are specifically for the lower-functioning child.

For Higher-Functioning Children:

- Ask the teacher for a list of important facts and definitions that he will need to know for the test.

- Write the facts on two index cards: half of the fact on the first card, and the other half on the second card.

- Write the definitions on two index cards: write the word on the first card, and the definition on the second card.

- Work on only two or three card sets a night. If the child learns quickly, you can increase the number of cards, but it's best to start slowly.

- Have your child read the facts and definitions on the cards three times.

- Place the cards on the table, words on one side of the table and definitions on the other side. Have your child match the word card to the definition card. Introduce new cards on the table for repetitive review, but don't exceed a total of five card sets at any one time.

- Rotate the five card sets until all the cards have been used at least once. This will reinforce what the child has already learned, but keep it from being overwhelming.

- Reward correct responses.

- Prepare for a multiple-choice test by placing one definition card and four word cards on the table. Have the child choose the correct word card.

- Prepare for a true-or-false test by matching the words with either their correct or incorrect definition. Have the child tell you if it is true or false. (Do this only after he has mastered all the definitions; doing it too early could confuse him.)

- Prepare for a fill-in-the-blank test by placing only the definition card on the table, and have your child say or write the correct response.

- Prepare for an essay test by placing the word card down, and have him write the definition.

- Prepare for a labeling test by placing an unlabeled map or diagram on the table. Make small labels, and work on correctly placing two new labels a night until the child can do them all.

- For a deeper understanding of the underlying academics, check out my textbooks designed for the autistic learner. They use pictures and hands-on activities while building language skills.

For Lower-Functioning Children:

- Use photographic flash cards to build vocabulary for younger students.

- Buy a book on the basics of Applied Behavior Analysis. See resource list at the back of this book.

- Label objects around the house if your child is a reader.

- Act out verbs. Make it a game in which your child gets to order you to jump, clap, skip, etc.

- Place your hand over his to help your child do what you want. Say the action word while you act it out.

- Place your child's hand on an object and tell him its name.

- Take photos of the people whom they see frequently. Review the cards before meeting those people.

- Take photos of the places your child goes on a regular basis and turn them into flash cards.

- Place the photos on a board or strip to make a picture itinerary of the places your child will be going and the people he will meet. Children with autism do better if they can prepare themselves for what is about to happen.

Chapter 10

The
Bathroom

Your child's problems with hygiene will be obvious to his teachers and, depending on his age group, to his peers, as well. They will be able to tell if his teeth are not getting brushed, his hair washed, or if he has not bathed. It's hard to admit failings in this area, but please ask for help from the school if you need it.

- Have your child play with warm, soapy water in a bucket or small tub outside if he doesn't like the bathtub. Give him toys to play with, and make the experience an enjoyable one.

- Let your child play with warm, soapy water in the sink. Put soap bubbles on his head as a game. Let him see himself in the mirror with bubbles on his head. Put some bubbles on your own head.

- Spread a damp facecloth over your spread-out hand to create Face Monster. Playfully chase your child around the house, calling out "Face Monster!" Have the Face Monster swallow your child's face.

- Draw a bath with warm, soapy water. Put in his favorite toys and just let him play.

- Take a damp facecloth and create Bath Monster. Wash his tickle spots: under his chin, behind his ears, under his armpits, and his belly button.

- Use the damp facecloth to wet his hair. Make this part of the Bath Monster routine.

- Put a small amount of shampoo between your hands. Lather it up with a small amount of water. Start placing the lather on his head.

- Have the child lie down in the tub. Gently lap the water up to rinse off the shampoo.

- Have the child lean partly back and use the bucket to rinse the shampoo off.

- Get a hose attachment for the showerhead, and carefully direct the spray.

- Use a cloth over his eyes if you have no choice but to use a straight dunk in the bucket.

- Check out the dry shampoos often used in nursing homes for patients who cannot be bathed.

- Wipe your child's teeth with a wet terry-cloth washrag if he will not let you brush his teeth. The rough texture will help clean his teeth and protect your fingers if he bites.

- Give him a clean, wet toothbrush to put in his mouth.

- Try an electric toothbrush. He might enjoy the sensory stimulation.

- Use non-fluoride toddler toothpaste until he learns how to spit.

- Have spitting contests in the sink. This is one skill he will enjoy learning!

- Relax about toilet training. It's going to be a long time before he learns, but most children eventually do learn.

- Diapers are available through medical assistance with a prescription for incontinence.

- Watch to see if your child soils his diaper at certain times of the day.

- See if he has a favorite spot to visit when he needs to go. This is a sign that he's aware something is coming.

- Give your child water to drink if he is constipated. Water quickly stimulates the digestive system to help the body push.

- Get behind your child if he has smeared feces on himself. Put two fingers under each armpit; they are usually the cleanest spots, and you can control his arms as you guide him to the bathtub.

- If your child has had a soiled diaper on for a while, soak him in the tub to coax off any dried feces. It is gentler on his tender skin than wiping it firmly.

- Teach potty-training skills in small chunks: pulling down his pants, sitting on the potty for a few seconds. Build the skills slowly. Reward each small step.

- Show your child potty videos and read the potty books. Have the same-gender parent or sibling model appropriate toileting.

- Write out the steps if your child can read, or make a picture schedule for a child who can't read.

- If your child finds the pressure from a full diaper comforting, use looser diapers on him.

- Read *Toilet Training Individuals with Autism and Related Developmental Disorders* by Maria Wheeler.

- When your child can use the toilet, but lacks the incentive to do so, switch to cloth underwear. The feeling of wet, soiled clothing is unpleasant. (See the Broom Closet chapter for cleaning tips.)

Chapter 11

The Broom Closet

When you have a child with autism, you develop a disregard for material possessions that would be the envy of a medieval monk. You look upon all objects with an eye for what your child could do to them. Sigh, and move on. This section contains tips for keeping your remaining possessions clean and in working order.

- Use a carpet cleaner designed for pets when cleaning urine or fecal matter from your carpet.

- Soak the remaining stain with water and press a disposable diaper into the wet area. The diaper pulls the dirty water up and removes any remaining residue.

- Use a diaper wipe to clean surfaces if you have run out of cleaner.

- Check doorjambs, door knobs, and light switches for any possible fecal matter, as well as the walls at the child's arm level. Check any furniture he might have sat on.

- Spray mattresses with the pet carpet cleaner. Wipe with the grain of the fabric. If you wipe against it, the fabric tears easily. Soak any remaining stain and press with a disposable diaper.

- Air the mattresses outside to remove any remaining smell.

- Clean your bathtub drain with Drano. The fecal matter can catch in a hair clog and smell.

- Place towels over your child's bed if he has an upset stomach—especially over his upper legs and groin area. A sick child will often sit up and throw up in that exact spot.

- Place towels on the floor around a sick child's bed.

- Put a pull-up on your sick child, even if he is toilet trained. The diarrhea may catch him by surprise.

- Get wrought-iron lamps. They are difficult to break or dismantle, and they still look attractive.

- Get overhead lights. Consider recessed lighting if your child likes to hang from the lights.

- Watch the plumber the first time you have something stuck in the toilet. Have them teach you how to use an auger. Buy one.

- Fix a dryer door that has been bent by the weight of your child by checking just above the hinges. There will be a bulge there from where the interior part of the hinge pushed against the door. Take a hammer and flatten it so it is even with the rest of the dryer. Duct-tape the door shut.

- Sprinkle salt on raw eggs that fall on the floor. It breaks up the connectivity and allows you to clean it up more quickly.

- Attach bookcases and curio cabinets to the wall. Your child could tip them over onto himself or others if he climbs up the shelving.

- Tie the handles of a curio cabinet together with a ribbon tied in a square knot that will only get tighter if pulled upon.

- Put away anything you don't want broken.

- Assign easy chores for your child to do. The following tips are suggestions.

- Place the pillow on his bed after you have made it. Pull up the comforter after you've straightened the sheets.

- Smooth out the wrinkles on the bed after you've pulled up the sheets.
- Pull up the sheets and blankets.
- Strip the sheets when they need to be washed.
- Carry his dirty clothes to the hamper after he has changed into his pajamas.
- Sort the laundry by color.
- Drop the tablet or your pre-measured detergent into the washing machine.
- Add the dryer sheets.
- Pick up toys and put them in the toy box.
- Pick up trash and put it in the trash can.
- Empty any small trash baskets into a large trash bag.
- Hand you the dirty dishes.
- Place the dirty dishes in the dishwasher.
- Wash or dry the dishes.
- Hand you the clean dishes to put away.

Chapter 12

The Front Door

Good manners are essential for a child with autism, so give him a script for what is appropriate to say in different social situations. Interactions with others are stressful, but if children are polite, people love it, and will give them tremendously positive feedback. Your child's social confidence and acceptance will rise!

- Be unfailingly polite when interacting with your child. He learns language in word groups. He will learn, "May I have some ... please?" if you say it that way. He might not know what each word means, but he knows that this is how you ask for something you want.

- Say "Thank you" whenever he hands you something, or does something you asked him to do.

- Say "Great job!" or "That's awesome!" whenever you look at a project he is working on.

- Ask, "Are you all right?" every time he falls down or cries. Seeing another child hurt or crying can be very stressful. Some children with autism may start crying or, worse, laughing, when another child is crying. Learning the appropriate thing to say gives your child a way to deal with the situation and teaches him to show concern for others.

- Make comic or picture strips to illustrate when you would use common phrases.

- Teach him to look at you by saying, "Look at me." Place an M&M between your eyes. He gets the M&M when he looks at you.

- Make a game out of "look at me" and "look away."

- Smile when he looks at you. Put as much love as you can into your eyes.

- See if he is turning his ear to you slightly when he looks away from you. Sometimes a child with autism, if he wants to understand what you are saying, looks away in order to decrease sensory input to the brain. He can concentrate better if all he is doing is listening.

- Do not make him look at you when you are angry.

- Teach him to say, "I'm sorry," when you are angry. Change your mood immediately upon hearing it. It is vital to teach your child how to handle angry people whom he will meet in the world. His lack of social skills may accidentally offend a classmate or someone in authority.

- Say, "Bless you!" when he sneezes. Have him say, "Bless you!" when you or someone else sneezes.

- Greet him with "Good morning, (his name)" or "Hello, (his name)." Teachers will train him to do that in school. Hearing it at home will give him a head start.

- Wave when you say "Good-bye." Help him to wave back. It will help him deal with separation if he has something to do.

Chapter 13

The Back Door

Some children with autism are born "escape artists." This is a particularly important issue because they have little sense of what is dangerous. Some of the following tips may be against the fire code in your area. Please check. All these tips do is buy you time. Time to get to him before he leaves, and time to mature until he can recognize danger.

- Put a chain lock near the *top* of your doors.
- Install a door chime or bell that's activated when the door is opened.
- Put a buzzer alarm mat in the doorway.
- Put a wooden fence around your yard. Plastic ones are more easily broken, and chain-link fences are full of footholds for small feet!
- Put chicken wire around the inside of the fence to eliminate any potential footholds.
- Staple the chicken wire to the fence.
- Use tent pegs to secure the base of the chicken wire.
- Keep recent photos available to show the police in case your child gets lost.

- Take regular walks with your child around your neighborhood. Introduce him to any neighbors you meet on your walk. Describe the house that you live in. People often forget numbers, but remember descriptions.

- Walk the same route every time. If he does leave the house by himself, he will probably follow that route.

- Pay attention to what interests him in the neighborhood, and check those places first if he has "escaped."

- Check up in the trees, especially evergreen trees. They have lots of low branches that are easily climbed!

- Place a dog tag with his name, the word *autism*, and your cell phone number in the laces of his shoes.

- Pray. Remember that even Mary and Joseph lost Jesus for three days. It can happen to anyone.

Part Two

The Child
with Autism
in the Community

~

Chapter 14

The Playground

The playground is the easiest social outing. The main obstacles are that autistic children do not understand how to interact with their peers, and their lack of the physical skills needed to master the playground equipment. Nevertheless, a playground is a good first step toward social interaction. There, the child with autism can observe typical play and feel little or no pressure to join in.

At first, go to the playground when it is not crowded. Your child will have a chance to explore the area without feeling pressure to participate in social interactions, or experiencing the sensory stimuli of a fully packed and noisy playground. Once your child is comfortable at the playground, you can go at busier times.

- Use the "little children" swings to hold your child securely while he learns to hold on and gets used to the swinging sensation. When it becomes evident that he enjoys the swinging motion, you can move up to the regular swings.

- Swing gently on the regular swings until your child consistently holds on.

- Teach the pumping motion when your child is still. Hold his legs out in front and say "Front." Push his legs back and say, "Back."

- Demonstrate the pumping motion while saying, "Front" and "Back."

- Push your child on the swings saying "Front" and "Back." The pumping motion takes a long time to learn, but make it fun— and don't give up!

- Stop the teaching exercise and swing as usual if your child gets stressed. The focus should be on his having fun outside the home.

- Go down a wide, straight slide with your child. Hold him between your legs and say, "That was fun!" Do this several times.

- Go down the slide first, and then encourage your child to come to you.

- Start with a small slide. A child with autism goes down a ladder facing *outward,* which can be dangerous.

- Teach your child how to back down a ladder. Have a helper go up the ladder first and stop at the top. Your child will go up next. You stay behind your child. To start back down, pick up your child's foot and put it on the next-lower rung. The helper should then back down as well, forcing your child to descend. Praise your child with each step he retreats. Reward him when he reaches the bottom.

- Do not go up the ladder if your child is descending while facing outward. He may jump into your arms or hug you, and tip you backward in the process! Stay at the bottom of the ladder with your feet firmly planted on the ground, ready to catch your child if he should fall.

- Remember what your child is wearing before you enter a fun fort. It's easy to lose a child in the wooden structures.

- Stay in visual contact with your child. Even if the playground has only one entrance, park benches are often placed against the walls. A child could easily exit without your knowing it.

- Bring snacks and drinks for your child. Other children's food is often in plain sight, and can be a great temptation.

- Be aware that a child chasing a duck or goose may follow it into the water.

Chapter 15

The Fast-Food Restaurant

Being able to eat at a fast-food restaurant as a family is essential if you are ever going to leave the house for more than a day trip. The problems you will have to overcome are teaching him to wait in line for his food, finding foods your child will eat at any particular restaurant, and keeping him at the table once he is seated. A fast-food restaurant can be an excellent place to perfect his eating-out manners. You have much more control in getting your food at a fast-food restaurant. And you won't stand out as much as you might think, because typical children don't always behave in fast-food restaurants, either.

- Go through the drive-through and eat the meal at home. Find out what your child likes to eat, so he will be motivated to stay in the restaurant later.
- Go through the drive-through and eat in the car.
- Eat inside the restaurant at a non-busy time; this will give him practice in staying at the table.
- Have your child sit in a booth close to the window. Sit beside him so he can't get out—except by climbing over you.
- Cut the burger into quarters if your child tends to separate his food into all its different components. He is less likely to

separate bite-sized pieces. They are also easier for you to hold if you need to encourage him to eat.

- Bring a special activity bag that your child gets to play with only at the restaurant.

- Bring a timer, so your child will know how long he is expected to stay there.

- Have your child throw his trash in the proper receptacle.

- When you're ready to practice waiting, go to the restaurant with another adult at a non-busy time. This person will sit with your child at the table while you order food at the counter. Make sure he can see you in line.

- Go to the restaurant with your child at a non-busy time. Have him wait with you while you order the food. Go to the table with him.

- Gradually work up to visiting the restaurant at busier times. Once your child is confident about where he is and what he is doing, he will be able to handle more people.

- Be aware that an impulsive child may steal food off other people's tables. Keep a sharp eye out when walking through the restaurant.

- Practice ordering the food with your child. Once he has it memorized, let him give the order.

- Have your child give the money to the cashier. This will teach him that we exchange money for things that we want.

- If your child knows math, have him calculate the change.

- Order a pizza over the phone, but eat it at the restaurant. Let your child watch the workers making pizza as you eat.

- Order at the pizza parlor and sit where your child can see the food being made while you wait. Be sure to take his special activity bag.

- Move on to other fast-service establishments. Explain that the food is being made behind the wall. Hopefully, by this time, your child understands that the food will come.

- Order mild General Tso's chicken as a good first meal from a Chinese restaurant.

Chapter 16

The Mall

Shopping at the mall is a difficult but necessary skill that a child with autism needs to master if he is going to function in society. The main obstacles are coping with the sensory overload of so many sights, sounds, smells, and people; staying with the family; and learning not to handle the merchandise. It is better to teach this in a store where you can buy what he breaks, than it is in a friend's home, where he might break another child's most treasured trophy or toys.

- Attach a dog tag with your child's name, your name, your phone number, and the word *autism* to the inner laces of your child's shoe. This is particularly helpful if your child is nonverbal. If you always carry a cell phone, use that phone number. I would be reluctant to write my address where predators might see it.

- Write out a script for your child. "Who are you?" "Sam Labosh." "What's your phone number?" "555-5555." A child with autism will do better if he can see it written out.

- Practice these questions and answers at home.

- Go early, when the mall is open but the stores are not. It is usually open for walkers who want to exercise.

- Walk around the mall to familiarize your child with the building. Make a note of what is of particular interest to your child. If he runs off, check these places first.

- Expect to spend long periods of time going up and down escalators and stairs.

- Bring small pieces of candy. Give your child a reward for staying with you over a certain distance. Praise lavishly.

- Buy your child a snack when the stores open, and then go home.

- Have your child try the coin-operated rides.

- Go into a clothing store or another store where the objects are hard to break. Tell your child, "No touch" if he tries to grab something. Keep practicing until he gets the idea.

- On each trip, spend just a little more time at the mall.

- Buy his shoes at stores that let you select the shoes from boxes instead of having to wait for a shoe salesman.

- Until you are confident that your child will stay with you, bring a helper to keep track of your child while you look at merchandise for an actual shopping trip.

Chapter 17

The Barber or Hairdresser

The child with autism hates getting his hair cut, but a well-groomed appearance can help him better fit in with his peer group. The main obstacles are the child's oversensitivity to his hair being touched, the noisy clippers, and the long time he must sit still. (A huge benefit: Mastering these skills will be useful in other social situations.)

- Play with your child's hair. Pull up a hank of hair and hold it the way the hairdresser or barber will. Smile at your child and make it an affectionate game. Take care not to pull too hard, or he may resist when the hairdresser does it.

- Buy clippers. Let your child feel the vibration on his hand and get used to the noise at home.

- Take your child to a kids' hair salon that shows videos.

- Meet the person who will be cutting his hair before taking your child for the actual haircut. Explain that your child has autism, and describe any behaviors that might occur (e.g., grabbing the scissors). Ask the hairdresser if s/he has had any experience with other kids with autism. Does he or she seem confident? Kind? Empathetic? Patient?

- Fill his hands with his favorite candy. He will have to drop the candy to grab the scissors.

- Make an appointment so that the wait-time won't be too long.

- Explain to the hairdresser that your child has a hard time sitting still for long periods, and that speed is important.

- Don't get his hair washed at the salon until he is already comfortable with the rest of the process.

- Use a booster seat that holds your child securely and lets him feel safe.

- Hold your child in place and reassure him. If possible, get below him so he can see your face. Give him lots of praise.

- No matter how badly he does, give him a reward afterward. You want him to associate this activity with a treat afterward. If you get angry, he will avoid this particular activity at all costs!

- Schedule his haircuts on a regular basis. Try to get the same hairdresser every time, too. The more familiar he is with any situation, the better he will behave.

Chapter 18

The Grocery Store

Having your child learn to behave in the grocery store can be a huge stress-reducer—for both of you! Even parents with typical children dread these trips. The most important skill your child needs to learn is to *stay with the cart.* Trying to keep track of him while you're standing at the deli counter can be a nightmare.

- The first few times you move your child out of the grocery cart and are training him to walk beside it, have an assistant with you if at all possible. Your assistant could be an understanding friend or neighbor, or even one of his therapists. This assistant should bring him back to the cart every time he starts to wander off.

- Go to the grocery store at a non-busy time (if possible, avoid weekends, noontime, the hours when people are getting off work, and the day before holidays). There will be fewer people, less noise, and the wait time in the checkout line will be shorter.

- On your first trips to the store together, pick up just a few items, including your child's favorite food. You want this trip to be short, and your child's opportunity for success to be optimal. (In time, the assistant will no longer be needed, and you will be able to gradually move to longer grocery lists.)

• Get your child's favorite food first. Place it in the bottom center of the cart, in plain sight, but out of reach. He will want to keep in close visual contact with that item.

• Bring a small candy treat to give your child when he has stayed with the cart for an entire aisle.

• Be generous with your praise.

• Tell your child he can pick out one treat. If he wants something else, show him the first treat. Tell him, "We got this—you'll get the other treat next time." If he insists on the second item, get it, but put the first item back.

• Have your child help unload the groceries when you reach the register. As soon as the groceries are paid for, give him his treat and tell him what a good boy he is.

• Create a learning project. Take photos of the products you normally buy, and make a pictorial list for your child. Have him go to that item in the store. Write the names of the items on the back of the photos, and use them as flash cards.

• If your child is older, go to the self-scanning checkout aisle and have him practice putting items into the bag while you scan.

• Later, when you feel he is ready, have him practice scanning the items himself.

• Mastering these tasks can result in a great deal of self-esteem for him. As difficult as they may be to learn initially, once he has mastered them, a child with autism—like everyone else— enjoys feeling competent and appreciated. Give him lots of positive feedback for a job well done.

Chapter 19

The Movie Theater

Going to a movie with a child with autism may seem like a pipe dream, but your child *can* learn to enjoy the experience. The primary obstacles are fear of the dark, the noises, upsetting images, and having to sit for a long time. I always go to nearly empty matinees during the training process, and the other people in the theater have always been fine with it. I was more concerned than they were!

- Have your child watch his favorite DVD or video in an increasingly dark room. You should start with all the lights on. Next, eliminate the lights closest to the TV. Gradually reduce the lighting until there is only a small light at the back of the room. This mimics the lighting in a movie theater: a dark room with a lighted projector in the rear.

- Tell your child that you are pretending to be in a theater. You should sit next to him and watch the video. Make it a fun time.

- Slowly turn up the volume, as well. In movie theaters the sound tends to be quite loud, so your child needs to be gradually acclimated to a higher level of noise.

- Give your child popcorn and his favorite drink while the two of you are watching the movie.

- If your child gets up and won't return to his seat, turn off the video. Restart it when he comes back, and give him small pieces of his favorite candy over short intervals of time for staying in his seat. If he just won't sit, let it go. This is not the place for a power struggle!

- Go to a local movie theater and explain that your child has autism and you would like him to see what a theater looks like inside. Let him look around, and explain what everything is (the posters, fountains, concession stand, ticket-taker, and the usher—if there is one—etc.).

- Pick a very gentle movie—one that isn't likely to feature many loud noises or explosions. You may never get your child back into a theater again if he gets terrified early on.

- Take him to a matinee of the movie when it's at the end of its run. The theater will be practically empty!

- Go to the movie a little late, to avoid the previews. Previews tend to show the most stimulating scenes of other movies, and can frighten your child. Also, previews are almost always louder than the actual movie.

- Buy your child a tub of popcorn and place it on his lap. Buy him a soda and hold it for him while he eats the popcorn. Buy a large box of small candies, and when the popcorn and soda run out, give your child the candy for staying put.

- If your child wants to leave the theater, take him to the bathroom. Ask him if he wants to go back in. If he doesn't, then it's time to go home. Praise him for the time he stayed.

- Expect to leave before the end of the show. It can take several tries before your child will sit through an entire movie.

Chapter 20

Church

Many parents deeply desire to pass on their faith to their child with autism. This faith is often what sustains the parents through the rough times. Even a nonverbal child can learn aspects of your faith through visual means and hands-on activities.

- Say the basic prayers of your faith every night with your child at bedtime. Children with autism have good auditory memory, even if understanding is lacking, and learn language in phrases. One day your child may surprise you by saying the entire prayer.

- Watch religious videos for children, such as *Veggie Tales*. Children with autism are visual learners, and will remember what they see and hear on videos.

- Have your child listen to religious songs. Many children, including typical children, remember words that are set to music better than words that are merely spoken.

- Let your child play with plastic statues or action figures of people important to your faith. Tell him their names and briefly explain something about them. (Hint: Plastic statues last longer than action figures.)

- Play a matching game with pictures of people who are important to your faith.

- Get simple books containing faith stories that have been passed down for generations. These stories connect your child culturally with others of your faith.

- Use felt boards to illustrate religious stories. Let your child place the people in the scene.

- Have them assemble puzzles with religious themes.

- Take photographs of everything in your house of worship. Cut the main object out of the photo, place it on a flashcard, and laminate it.

- Using the photos, write a social story about what happens during the service.

- Let your child examine the church when no one is around. Whenever you come to an object that you've photographed, show him the photograph and say the object's name.

- Give your child a photograph, and have him go to the object. If he doesn't remember what it is, show him the photograph and say the object's name. Let this be fun and games time.

- Have your child sit in the narthex or lobby, or sit in the "cry room" if it's not full of noisy children.

- During the service, have your child play with a quiet toy, such as a calculator. Sit up front, where your child can see what is going on. It will also lessen his social anxiety if he doesn't see a lot of people in front of him, as he would if you sat in the back of the church.

- Let your child follow along in the missal, program, or bulletin.

- Tell your child how long the service will take.

- For Catholics, GLEA (God's Love Embraces Autism) has a pictorial social story of the Mass with written responses, titled "We Go to Mass." Contact the Diocese of Pittsburgh (disabilities@dio-pitt.com) for infromation about GLEA.

- *The Rose Fitzgerald Kennedy Program to Improve Catholic Education for Children and Adults with Mental Retardation* provides twelve years of religious-education lesson plans. It was written by the Diocese of Pittsburgh and produced by the Joseph P. Kennedy, Jr. Foundation.

- Start a small religious education class in your church specifically for children with developmental disabilities. Use the Rose Kennedy Curriculum or *The Child with Autism Learns about Faith* (visit www.FHautism.com for more info).

Chapter 21

The Amusement Park

Going to an amusement park can eventually be a very enjoyable experience for children with autism, but the noises and crowds can be overly stimulating at first. The main considerations are the crowds, which rides to choose, then waiting in line to access them.

- Make sure that your child is already comfortable at the playground before trying an amusement park.

- Buy your tickets ahead of time. Tickets are usually available at a discount at your local AAA. They are also available through special promotions at local grocery stores or drugstores. Having tickets in hand will cut down on the wait-time to get into the park.

- Try to schedule your first trip to a park during a weekend in the spring or fall; it will usually be less crowded then. Once your child is comfortable with the park, you can go at busier times.

- Wear a fanny pack instead of a backpack or purse. You'll get through security faster, and you'll have both hands free for your child. Have another member of the party carry other items, and meet them inside.

- Go to Guest Relations and explain that your child has autism and has difficulty waiting in line. Bring a doctor's note (some parks require it; others don't). They will give you a pass that allows you quicker (though not immediate) access to the rides. The access is usually through the exit or the handicapped area. They will give you a brochure explaining the procedure for each ride.

- Take the card instead of the bracelet if a choice is offered. A child with touch sensitivities will not be able to tolerate a bracelet.

- Cut the bracelet with a key if your child is having a major meltdown. The bracelets are difficult to unsnap, and because of the security checks, you will have no other sharp objects available.

- Start with the monorail if the park has one. It's a smooth ride, and gives your child a good overall view of the park. You can point out the various rides you want to try.

- Sit with your arm around your child toward the back of the steam train. This will get you away from the steam engine's whistle and the general noise.

- Take the observation tower that slowly climbs into the air and then rotates, to give your child another overview of the park.

- Sit with your child on the kiddie rides that go up in the air. These rides are early favorites for a child with autism.

- Try the Mini-Himalaya if the park has one. My son surprised me by putting his arms up in the air.

- Know your child before putting him on the spinning cups. If he tends to whirl repetitively, he will love it! But some children may be sensitive to the spinning motion.

- Have your child try the large slides with the burlap bags to sit on. My children rode them over and over again.

- Beware of the merry-go-round! It can overwhelm the senses of a child with autism. The music is loud. Part of the world around them (outside the merry-go-round) seems to be moving, but other parts around them seem to stay in the same spot. They are also being moved up and down while straddling an unfamiliar object. You need to take this slowly!

- Sit on the bench seats that are usually found on merry-go-rounds. This cuts off part of the view and gets your child used to the music and the constantly changing view. You will also have more control over your child if there's a problem.

- If the bench seat went well, you can move to a stationary horse. This will get your child accustomed to balancing himself on a horse. And if he tries to get off, it's easier to hold on to him.

- If the stationary horse went well, you can try the moving horse next. Stand on the "outside" of the horse. If your child decides to bolt, he will go to the outside, away from the carousel. You will be able to catch him and unbuckle the belt. If you are to the inside of the horse, it will be between you and your escaping child. If he manages to get his inside leg over the horse, he'll be hanging by the belt.

- Watch out for rides where you will get splashed. If your child does not like the shower, he will probably not like getting splashed, and may try to escape.

- Bring a spare set of clothes for accidents, or if your child's clothes get wet.

- Before putting your child on a ride where he will get splashed, try putting him under a hose sprinkler or shower at home.

- Avoid dark, loud, or scary rides.

- Bring your child's favorite foods if he has taste sensitivities. Otherwise, hamburgers, cheeseburgers, hot dogs, and pizza are readily available in the park.

Chapter 22

Sports and Sporting Events

Sports are important to your child's social life at school. It's good to help him participate, even as a spectator. Participating in sports builds self-confidence, improves motor coordination, and often builds social skills as well.

- Avoid large sporting events that can be noisy with little warning. Fans jumping up and screaming can be alarming to a child with autism. Open-ended stadiums are quieter than closed stadiums or indoor arenas.

- Start with minor-league baseball games. The stadiums are smaller, quieter, and the activities are often family-oriented. Most of these venues offer enjoyable activities for children between innings.

- Watch different sports on TV to learn what appeals to your child most.

- Visit a local children's soccer game. Let your child watch from the bleachers or walk around the sidelines to see what is going on.

- Buy him sodas and/or bring some of his favorite foods.

- Check with Special Olympics or Easter Seals to learn what sporting opportunities are available for children with disabilities.

- Ask your local school about private swimming lessons. If you intend to go to a pool or a beach as a family, it's essential that your child learn enough swimming skills to be safe in the water. Always put flotation devices on the child.

- Buy a stationary bike and a treadmill for the house. These are good for your child's physical fitness, but they can also be dangerous, so they require constant supervision.

- Visit a roller-skating or ice-skating rink. Either enroll your child in private lessons or, if you are proficient, teach him yourself.

- Take your child to a local ski resort with an inner-tube run. No experience is required.

- Take your child skiing as long as you are proficient enough to control both yourself and your child. Have your child ski at your side and both of you hold your poles horizontally in front of you. Do this until your child learns the basic wedge position and learns to control his speed. This may take a long time.

Chapter 23

The
Doctor

Doctor's visits can be difficult. The major problems are the waiting time to see the doctor, the occasional multiple shots, and all the fascinating objects in the examination room that your child should not touch.

- Apply for medical assistance. Children with autism are usually eligible, regardless of the parents' income.

- Ask around the autism community to find a doctor who is experienced in dealing with children with autism. An experienced doctor is more likely to tolerate and understand your child's behavior. He or she will also be more current on the latest developments. In general, a younger doctor is likely to know more about autism than an older doctor does. That is because, until recently, autism was considered so rare that it was given little coverage in medical school curriculums. Even pediatricians were not previously well informed.

- Look for a doctor who is flexible, and has confidence in you as a parent. Children with autism exhibit unusual behaviors. If you think a particular treatment is helping a particular behavior, your doctor should trust your observations. You are the expert here.

- Find a doctor who will look at and talk to your child, even if your child is nonverbal. Avoid a doctor who talks only to you and ignores your child except when performing the physical examination.

- Bring your child to the doctor's office at a time when the child doesn't have an appointment and the office isn't crowded. Let him get familiar with the waiting area and, if possible, an exam room. A reasonable doctor who is experienced in autism would allow this.

- Read the child a social story about what happens at the doctor's office. Look for one that uses photographs and simple language.

- When you go to an appointment, bring an activity bag in case there is a long wait.

- If you can, bring another adult to look after your child's needs while you talk to the doctor. Ask the doctor to limit the initial physical exam to no longer than absolutely necessary. For the first visit, the doctor might do no more than talk to your child and try to set him at ease.

- Ask the nurse if she can hold off putting you in the exam room until just before the doctor gets there. The shorter the wait time, the less the chances are that your child will act out.

- If your child gets bored with the activity bag, let him play with the water in the sink.

- Let your child leave the room with the other adult if the doctor is through with him but still needs to discuss something with you.

- Ask for an additional nurse if your child is receiving multiple shots. They can be administered simultaneously on both legs.

- Ask if the shots can be given last, if possible, so you can leave quickly afterward.

- Ask your doctor if you can give your child a mild sedative before a visit involving multiple shots or invasive procedures.

Chapter 24

The Pharmacy and Medicine

Getting traditional medicines down a child's throat can be difficult. Children with autism are not good at swallowing pills and are not easily persuaded to swallow anything they don't like. There are, however, some strategies to make it easier on your child, and some new ways of dispensing medicine that are available from compounding pharmacists.

- Learn if the pill comes in a quick-dissolve tablet.

- Have a compounding pharmacist make the medicine into a flavored lozenge. Its texture is similar to that of a Gummy Bear.

- Secure the medicine safely when you get home, because your child might think that it's candy!

- Have liquid medicine flavored by the pharmacist.

- Have a compounding pharmacist make the medicine into a transdermal gel that can be rubbed on the child's skin.

- Have a compounding pharmacist make Allithiamine into a gel that can be rubbed on the soles of the child's feet. (Note: it smells like garlic.)

- Have a compounding pharmacist make Secretin into a frozen gel that can be rubbed on the child's wrists.

- Some drugstores will deliver medicines that need to be compounded; it can save an extra trip to the pharmacy.

- Hide regular pills in chunky peanut butter. Your child will have a hard time distinguishing the pill from the peanuts. (Naturally, if your child has peanut allergies, don't do this.)

- If your child tends to spit out medicines, place his chin in the palm of your hand, lift his head up, and blow in his face. This forces him to swallow.

- Give your child a piece of chocolate to eat before giving him a bitter-tasting medicine. Chocolate's strong flavor masks bitter ones.

- Give your child yogurt or milk products before giving him medicine. Milk coats the tongue and throat so your child won't taste the medicine as much. (Obviously, this is not for children on a dairy-free diet.)

- Have a favorite candy treat in sight and ready to give him when your child has to take a bitter-tasting medicine.

- Mix liquid medicine with Kool-Aid. Juice works quite well with some medicines—but not with others, because of its acidic nature. Check with your doctor.

- Sprinkle powders over ice cream with nuts. (Of course, not for children with nut allergies or who are on a dairy-free diet.)

- Mix powders in applesauce.

- Mix powders in yogurt (again, not for those children who are on a dairy-free diet).

- ALL medicines should be taken on a trial basis. Some cold-medications can make some children hyperactive, and might cause drowsiness in others. Other medications can make children with autism aggressive. Watch carefully for side effects. Discontinue over-the-counter medicine if the side effects are worse than the symptoms being treated. With prescription medicines, call your doctor and describe the side effects.

Chapter 25

The Dentist

Good dental care is important. Some parents may have unpleasant memories of their own trips to the dentist–but dentistry has changed considerably. Advances in equipment and techniques make the process much less painful. And pediatric dentists, especially, offer a child-friendly environment that can put your child at ease.

- So find a pediatric dentist! They have the most experience with children with developmental delays.

- Take your child to the waiting room when he doesn't have an appointment. Let him explore the waiting area, and then go home.

- Make a list of your child's favorite DVDs. Many offices will play movies for their patients. You might want to bring one of your child's favorites from home, in case he doesn't like the one that is being shown.

- Read a social story with photographs about going to the dentist.

- Bring some of your child's favorite toys to distract him from the dental exam.

- In the first few visits, the dentist will often just look in your child's mouth and touch his teeth, followed by a gentle brushing.
- Tell your child that the dentist is counting his teeth. Many children with autism count everything, so counting teeth will make perfect sense to them.
- Children with autism may benefit from several visits to the dentist's office to acclimate them to the office routines, sounds, smells, and staff members.
- Have your child observe another, cooperative child during a non-invasive dental appointment. This works only if your child has an interest in what others are doing.
- Have your child practice opening his mouth at home. After a short wait, pop a candy in his mouth.
- Have your child practice opening his mouth while you put in a Popsicle stick. Move it around, as the dentist might. Give your child a reward for cooperating with this process.
- Have your child practice spitting by having a "spitting contest" at the sink. (He will love this!)
- The first time your child goes for a real cleaning, use a mild sedative until he gets used to the routine. Consult with your dentist.
- Be in the treatment room with your child to assist the dentist by keeping your child's hands away from the dentist and the instruments in your child's mouth.
- Give the dentist an opportunity to talk to your child. Your child may be more cooperative with a friendly dentist who looks at him while talking to him.

- Check to see if your child's dental surgery can be done in the hospital under general anesthesia. Insurance will usually pay if the dentist submits a letter of medical necessity. Dental insurance usually doesn't cover anesthesia unless the problem was caused by an accident, but medical assistance often will—even if the dentist doesn't accept medical assistance.

- Use nitrous oxide if your child can handle getting dental work done in the office.

Chapter 26

The Hospital

Hopefully, if your child needs to go to the hospital, there will be time to prepare him for the experience. Your role is to be an intermediary—helping the medical staff and your child understand each other.

- Inform the medical staff that your child has autism. Explain the degree to which the autism affects your child's ability to communicate and follow instructions.

- Tell them your child will rip the IV out of his arm if he gets the chance.

- Ask them to pre-sedate your child prior to inserting an IV or giving him anesthesia.

- Bring a small blanket or afghan to place on the floor. As the sedative takes effect, your child will become unsteady on his feet, and should be encouraged to play on the floor.

- Call the unit working with your child—the Day Surgery Unit, for example. Explain that he has trouble with long waits, and ask them to estimate the time until they will actually start to work with him.

- Take your child for a walk around the hospital and waiting area to familiarize him with the building.

- Ask if there are any forms that you can fill out ahead of time.

- Bring another adult with you to attend to your child while you are talking with the hospital personnel.

- Bring an activity bag (no food if there will be general anesthesia). Make it as fun a wait as possible.

- Try not to be anxious. Your child will not be calmer than you are.

- When your child starts coming out of the anesthesia, he will immediately grab for the IV. Make sure he doesn't harm himself trying to rip it out of his arm.

- In the pediatric ward, check to see what movies are available, and pick a favorite.

- Have someone your child knows stay with him the entire time. Of course, a parent is always best.

Chapter 27

The Library

Whether you actually take your child to the library or not depends greatly on your child. I have not taken Nicky to the library because, like so many children with autism, he loves the sound of ripping paper. Besides, despite being nonverbal, he is also noisy. We do, however, have a tremendous number of books at home. Most children's books are not suitable for him, because children with autism who don't understand language can't look at a picture and determine what is important.

Below is a list of children's publishers and authors whose books are most suitable for children with autism. (See the Resources section for more publishers, organizations, and websites.)

- Most picture books by DK Publishers are useful for building vocabulary, but they often have too many pictures on a page for a child with autism. It is often difficult for them to focus on a particular one. Use their smaller books.
- Scholastic has a series of Big Photo Books
- Jennifer Armstrong's books, especially *Sunshine, Moonshine*
- Stan & Jan Berenstain's early reader books, especially *Big Bear, Small Bear*

- Sandra Boynton's board books
- Norman Bridwell's Clifford series
- Helen Oxenburg's books, especially *I See, I Hear, I Touch*
- Molly Coxe's books, especially *Big Egg*
- P.D. Eastman's books, especially *Go Dog. Go!*
- Max Hayne's book *Ticklemonster and Me* is the best interactive play book. Our son Sam wanted us to read this together a couple of times every night for months.
- Yvonne Hookers' English translation of *One Green Frog*
- Mercer Mayer's book, *A Boy, A Dog, and A Frog*
- Peggy Rothman's book, *Good Night Gorilla*
- Richard Scarry's book, *Watch Your Step, Mr. Rabbit!* This is good if you demonstrate push, pull, and blow with your child while reading. Children enjoy the interaction. Mr. Scarry's word books have pictures that are too complicated for a child with autism.
- Dr. Seuss's book *Hop On Pop.* Dr. Seuss's other books can get too complicated very quickly. If your child is high-functioning, you can try them.

Chapter 28

Family Gatherings

Family gatherings can be the most difficult of events. The main challenges are your own expectations of how you and your child should behave, houses that are not child-proofed, and the high level of social interactions directed at your child. Also, children with taste sensitivities may not like any of the food that has been prepared.

- If possible, travel in two cars. If your child gets distressed, one parent can return home with him, and the rest of the family can stay. Feed your child ahead of time. A well-fed child is better behaved than a hungry one.

- Allay concerns that your child doesn't eat enough by explaining that he has already eaten.

- Bring food that your child will eat.

- If your child was not fed ahead of time, feed him in a separate room.

- Come early, before most of the people arrive. This lets your child get accustomed to the growing number of people, rather than being immediately plunged into a noisy crowd.

- Ask if you can remove certain breakables from your child's reach. If the host believes that you should just teach him not to touch things, explain that your child's brain development has been affected. People accommodate the blind and the deaf. Autism is not a result of bad parenting; it's a physical disability that can be only partially overcome by extensive therapy.

- Avoid homes where people refuse to accommodate you by doing even the simplest of child-proofing. This creates an inappropriate stress level on you and your child. They can visit you at your house.

- Pick a quiet place where you can go if your child becomes distressed.

- Bring your child's favorite toys or stuffed animals.

- Show your child pictures of individual family members, and teach him their names.

- Write out simple courtesy phrases and responses to questions. "How are you?" "I'm fine." "How is school?" "Good." Rehearse before you go.

- Take your child out for a walk if he gets distressed.

- Avoid your child's consumption of too much chocolate. A child with autism gets hyperactive from the sugar, and then emotionally fragile when his blood-sugar level drops. Let him have cookies, or other, less sugary treats, instead.

- Dress your child nicely. Forgiveness comes easier to kids who look cute.

- Let others watch your child if they volunteer. You need the break.

- Ask for help if you need it. People can't read your mind or anticipate your needs. Most people are glad to help if they are asked to do a specific task. "Please help me" is too general a statement. "Could you watch him while I eat?" is specific.

- Treasure any positive comments.

- Accept unwanted advice with "I'll have to think about that," and smile. They really are trying to help. People can't understand what it's like to live with autism until they experience it for themselves.

Resources

Children's Books & Other Materials

Children's books, teaching tools, and information about autism can be found in the following catalogs and websites.

- **Abilitations**
  Call: 800-850-8602 or visit *www.abilitations.com*

- **Autism-Asperger's Publishing Co.**
  Call: 800-913-897-1004 or visit *www.asperger.net*

- **Beyond Play**
  Call: 877-428-1244 or visit *www.beyondplay.com*

- **Different Roads to Learning**
  Call: 800-853-1057 or visit *www.difflearn.com*

- **Future Horizons, Inc.**
  Call: 800-489-0727 or visit *www.FHautism.com*

- **Jessica Kingsley Publications**
  Call: 011-442-078332301 or visit *www.jkp.com*

- **Mayer-Johnson Co.**
  Call: 800-588-4548 or visit *www.mayer-johnson.com*

- **Phat Art 4**
  Call: 866-250-9798 or visit *www.phatart4.com*

- **Pocket Full of Therapy**
  Call: 732-462-5888 or visit *www.pfot.com*

- **Special Needs Project**
  Call: 800-333-6867 or visit *www.specialneeds.com*

- **Super Duper Publications**
  Call: 800-277-8737 or visit *www.superduperinc.com*

- **The Center for Speech and Language Disorders**
  Call: 630-530-8551 or visit *www.csld.com*

- **Woodbine House**
  Call: 800-843-7323 or visit *www.woodbinehouse.com*

Autism Resources

- **The ARC of the United States**
  Call: 301-565-3842 or visit *www.thearc.org*

- **Autism Research Institute**
  Fax: 619-563-6840 or visit *www.autism.com*

- **Autism Society of America**
  Call: 800-3AUTISM or visit *www.autism-society.org*

- **Bubel/Aiken Foundation**
  Call: 224-430-0950 or visit *www.thebubelaikenfoundation.org*

- **Doug Flutie Jr. Foundation**
  Call: 866-3AUTISM or visit *www.dougflutiejrfoundation.org*

- **Unlocking Autism**
  Call: 866-366-3361 or visit *www.unlockingautism.org/main.asp*

Index

About the Authors

Kathy Labosh graduated from Penn State and worked as an economist. She is now a stay-at-home mom to Sam and Nicky, both of whom are children with autism. It became her mission to help others in similar situations. Kathy formed a Special Education Religious Class and is the author of a specialized curriculum for children with autism. She also received an Honorable Mention for Children's Fiction from *Writer's Digest*.

Kathy continues to work on additional books in The Child with Autism series, including *The Child with Autism Learns about Faith* (2011), *The Child with Autism Goes to Florida* (2011), and *The Child with Autism Learns MORE about Faith* (still in progress).

LaNita Miller is the author of beginning textbooks, and received her bachelor's degree in elementary education with a minor in early childhood education from Austin Peay State University and her master's degree in special education from George Peabody College, which is part of Vanderbilt University. She is currently completing her certification in behavioral analysis. She has over twenty years' experience in the special education classroom.